THANKSGIVING
CUT AND PASTE
WORKBOOK FOR PRESCHOOL

By MezzyArt Designs

FOR MORE VISIT US AT: **https://www.amazon.com/author/mezzyartdesigns**

THIS BOOK BELONGS TO:

THANKSGIVING CUTTING PRACTICE

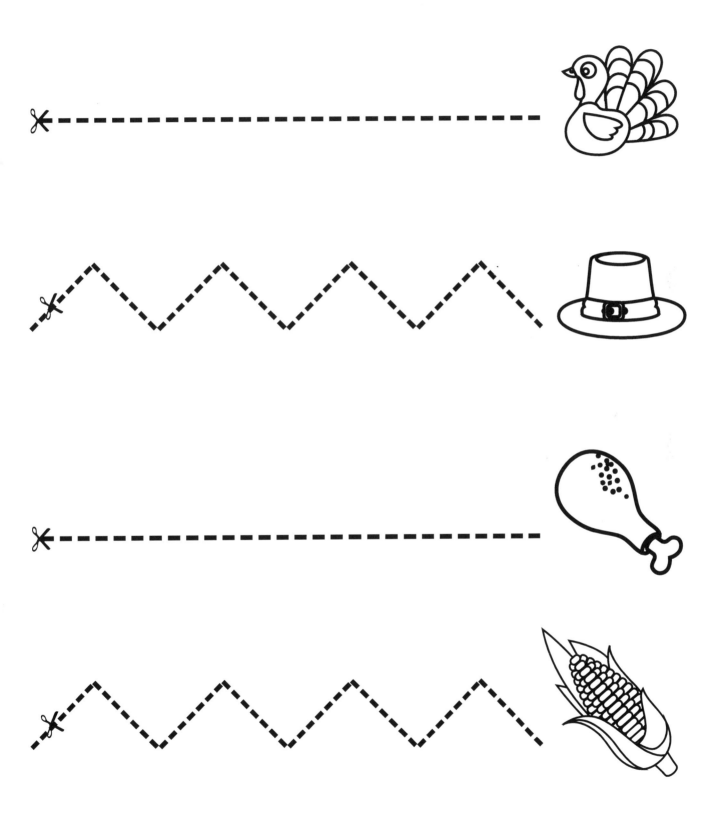

THANKSGIVING CUTTING PRACTICE

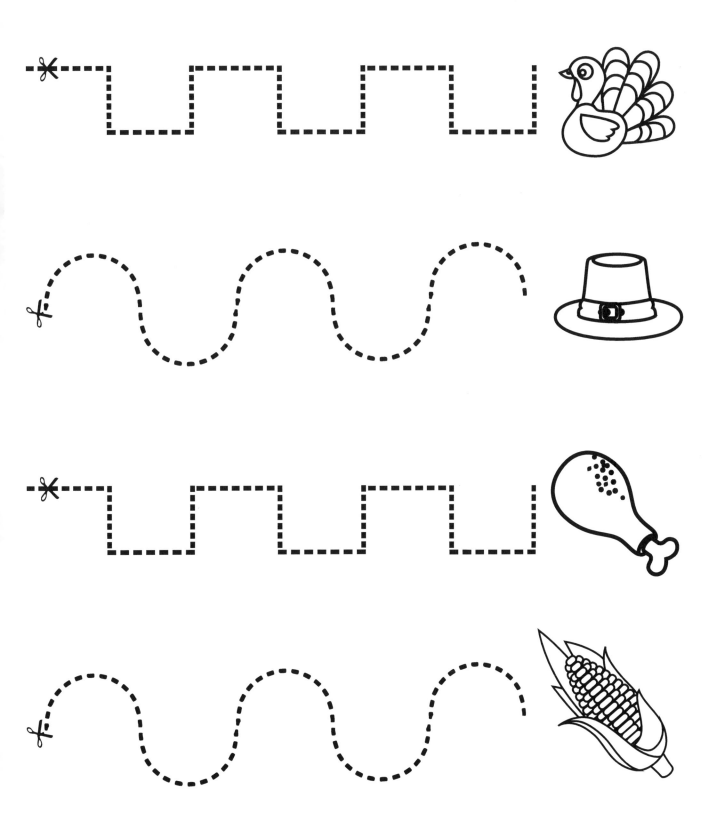

Cut And Paste Thanksgiving Fun Faces!

Cut And Paste Thanksgiving Fun Faces!

Cut And Paste Thanksgiving Fun Faces!

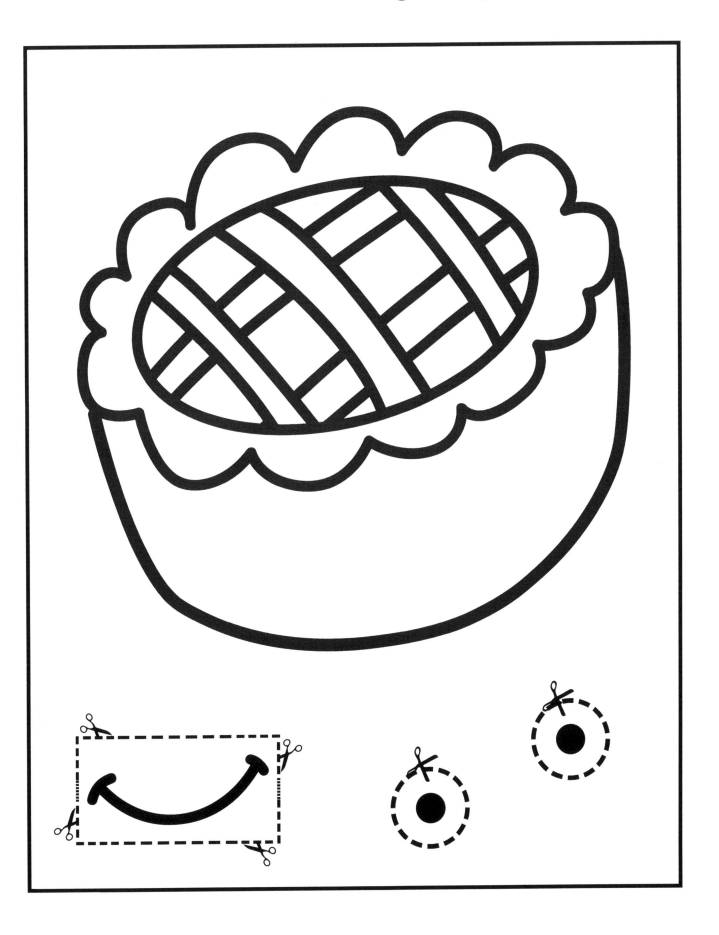

THANKSGIVING COUNTING

Count, Cut and Paste the Right Number!

THANKSGIVING COUNTING

Count, Cut and Paste the Right Number!

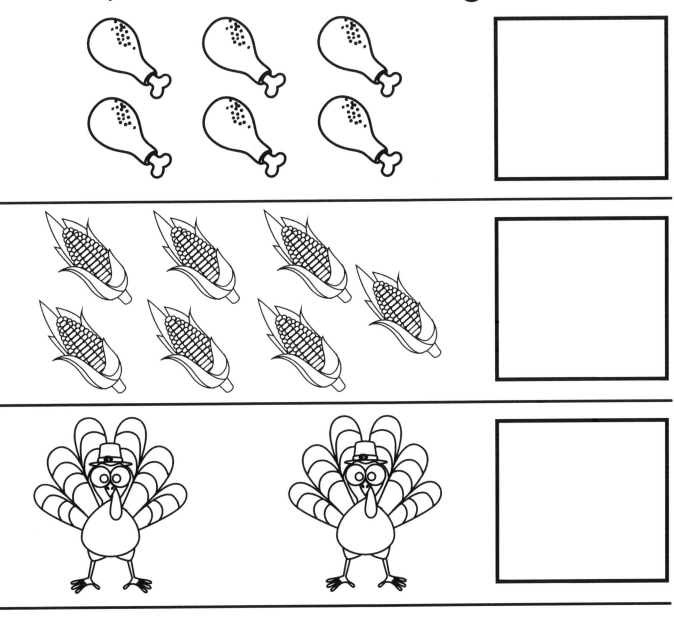

What Picture Comes Next?

What Picture Comes Next?

Color, Cut and Paste the Apples in Order from 1 to 10.

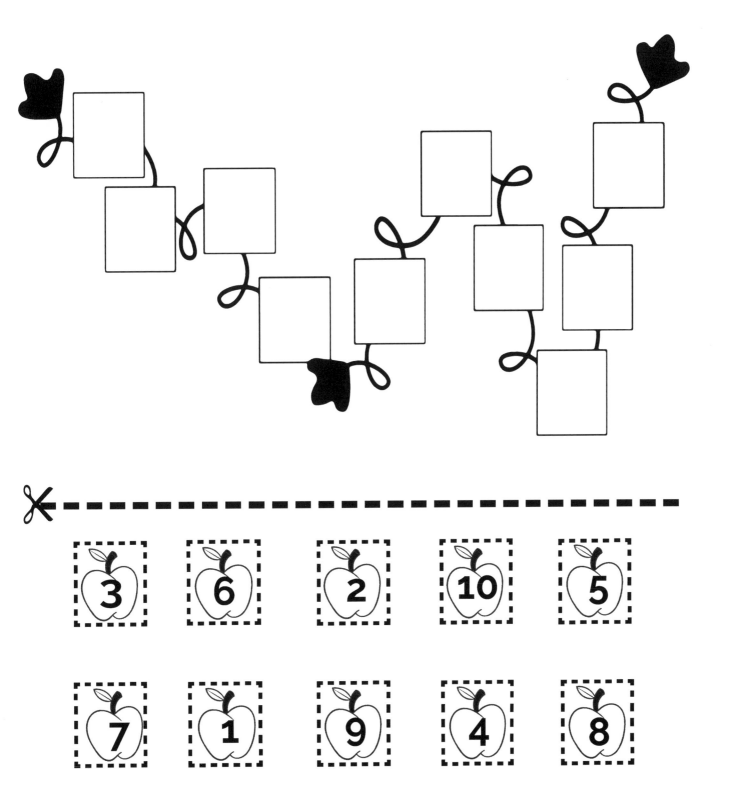

THANKSGIVING SHADOW MATCH

Cut and Paste pictures that match their shadows

THANKSGIVING SHADOW MATCH

Cut and Paste pictures that match their shadows

SMALLEST TO BIGGEST

Cut and Paste them in Order of smallest to biggest.

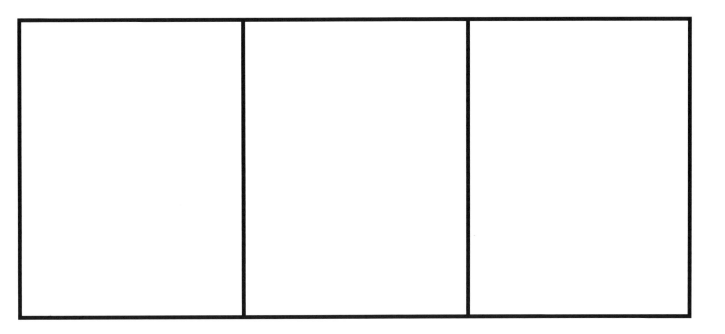

BIGGEST TO SMALLEST

Cut and Paste them in Order of biggest to smallest.

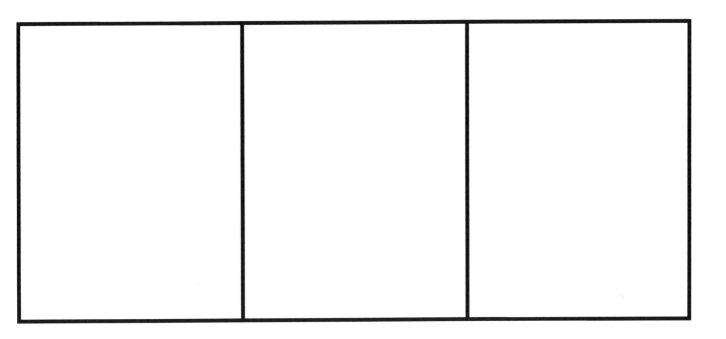

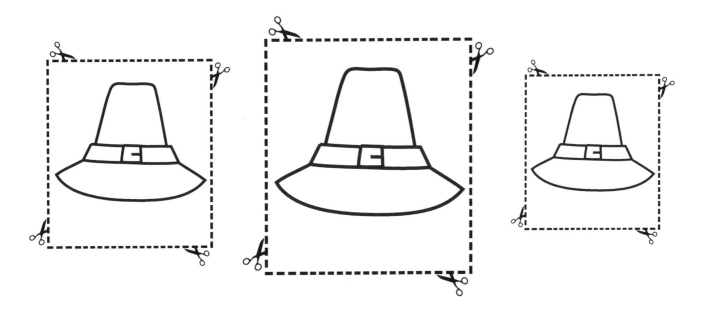

Cut and Paste inside the Right Box!

THANKSGIVING COLORING
COLOR AND CUT!

THANKSGIVING COLORING
COLOR AND CUT!

THANKSGIVING COLORING
COLOR AND CUT!

THANKSGIVING COLORING
COLOR AND CUT!

THANKSGIVING COLORING
COLOR AND CUT!

THANKSGIVING COLORING
COLOR AND CUT!

THANKSGIVING COLORING
COLOR AND CUT!

THANKSGIVING COLORING
COLOR AND CUT!

THANKSGIVING COLORING
COLOR AND CUT!

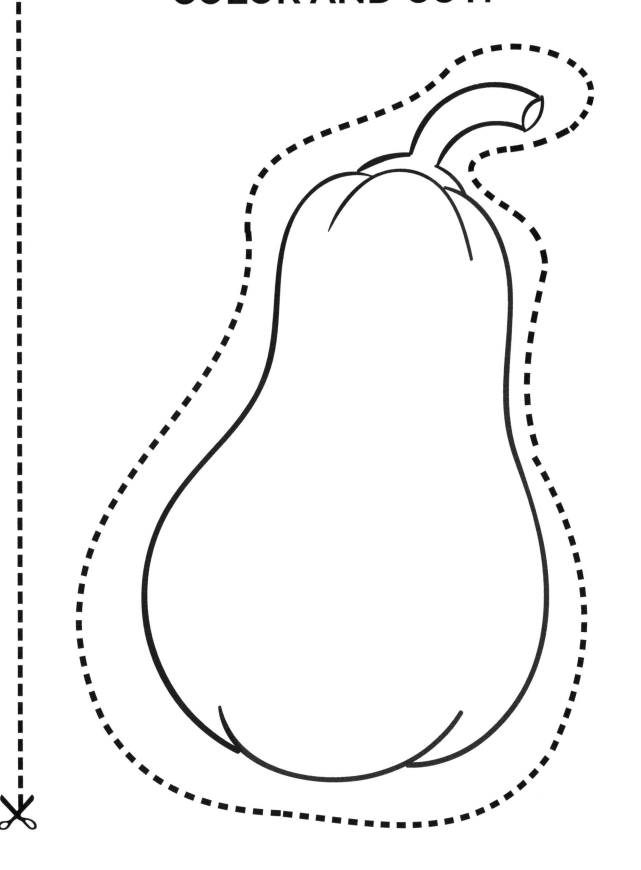

Made in United States
Orlando, FL
27 October 2024